THE DAUGHTER OF MAN

Miller Williams Poetry Series
EDITED BY PATRICIA SMITH

THE
DAUGHTER
OF
MAN

L. J. Sysko

The University of Arkansas Press
Fayetteville
2023

ISBN: 978-1-68226-230-6
eISBN: 978-1-61075-797-3

27 26 25 24 23   5 4 3 2 1

Manufactured in the United States of America

Designed by Liz Lester and Daniel Bertalotto
Cover illustration by Chloe McEldowney, *The Daughter of Man*, 2022
Cover design by Daniel Bertalotto

♾ The paper used in this publication meets the minimum requirements of
the American National Standard for Permanence of Paper for Printed
Library Materials Z39.48-1984.

Library of Congress Cataloging-in-Publication Data

Names: Sysko, L. J., author.
Title: The daughter of man / L. J. Sysko.
Description: Fayetteville: The University of Arkansas Press, 2023. | Series:
    Miller Williams poetry series | Summary: "The Daughter of Man, finalist
    for the 2023 Miller Williams Poetry Prize, follows its unorthodox heroine
    as she transforms from maiden to warrior—then to queen, maven, and
    crone—against the backdrop of suburban America. This collection
    confronts misogyny and violence, even as it bursts with nostalgia, lust,
    and poignant humor"—Provided by publisher.
Identifiers: LCCN 2022049637 (print) | LCCN 2022049638 (ebook) |
    ISBN 9781682262306 (paperback; alk. paper) | ISBN 9781610757973 (ebook)
Subjects: LCGFT: Poetry.
Classification: LCC PS3619.Y928 D38 2023 (print) |
    LCC PS3619.Y928 (ebook) | DDC 811/.6—dc23/eng/20221019
LC record available at https://lccn.loc.gov/2022049637
LC ebook record available at https://lccn.loc.gov/2022049638

Supported by the Miller and Lucinda Williams Poetry Fund.

CONTENTS

THE MAVEN

THE CRONE

SERIES EDITOR'S PREFACE

So you'd think, in the second year of my three-year term as Miller Williams Poetry Prize series editor, that I've clicked into a rhythm, undaunted by the hundreds of spectacular submissions flooding my inbox, and reliant on my stellar crew of screeners—all schooled in my exacting standards—to sift through all the goodness and present me with fifty stunners, from which I pluck the three clear winners, each one having risen to the top of the pile with the relentlessness of a north star.

Whew. *That* is overwritten.

But really—I'm not sure how folks picture this task, but it is, in turns, mystifying, exhilarating, and utterly impossible.

At the very heart of the difficulty is that age-old question, *What makes a good poem?* I have been confronted with that pesky query hundreds of times—served up by grade-schoolers, bookstore patrons, confounded undergrads, reading groups, festivalgoers, workshop participants, curious onlookers, byliners and bystanders, and folks just looking to make conversation when I tell them what I do. (And no—it's not just you—it took a *long* time before I was able to state "I am a poet" without tacking on something that felt legitimizing and more jobby, like ". . . oh, and a greeter at Walmart.")

What makes a good poem depends very much on who's doing the reading, when they're doing the reading, and issues and insight they brought to the table before starting to read. It's insanely subjective. At the beginning of my appointment as series editor (I almost said "at the beginning of my reign"—must be the scepter Billy Collins passed down to me), I was asked what kind of poems constituted the books I'd be looking for. Here's what I said:

> I love poems that vivify and disturb. No matter what genre we write in, we're all essentially storytellers—but it's poets who toil most industriously, telling huge unwieldy stories within tight and gorgeously controlled confines, stories that are structurally and sonically adventurous, and it's magic every time it happens. Simply put, when I read a poetry book, I want something to shift in my chest. I want my world to change.

That obviously was one bridge too far for a few folks, who wailed on social media—the primary forum for wailing—that my standards were merely unattainable. One incensed Tweeter (or is it "Tweeterer"?) was particularly riled by the "shift in my chest / world change" thing.

Who in their right mind believes that poetry can actually change the world? THIS world? Why are we teaching our younguns such lofty dribble? Why should the average poet submit a manuscript with absolutely no chance of shifting anything in this strange woman's chest? Alas, come down from that mountain, Madam Editor—can mere mortals get a break?

I want to repeat—and clarify—that good poetry should not leave you the same as when you came to it. I see that as a relatively simple ask on the part of the poet:

> *I have a story. It's a familiar story, but I'm going to tell it in a way you haven't heard before. I want to give the story to you. Take it with you. Live it.*
> *Now my story is part of your story.*

You'd be amazed at how many things I've felt that way about. The way Boo screeches "Kitty!" at the end of the film *Monsters, Inc.* A hard-rhymed scrawl by a sixth grader at Lillie C. Evans Elementary School in the Liberty City section of Miami. A poem written by a student of mine at Princeton—structured like an application form, it morphed into a heartbreaking and revealing piece about his being embarrassed by his aging mother. The children's book *Don't Let the Pigeon Ride the Bus!*. Everything ever penned by Gwendolyn Brooks. The one and only poem written by a reticent mumbler in my Staten Island Intro to Creative Writing class, because it was his one and only poem and he said he'd never write a poem at all. "Antarctica Considers Her Explorers" by Diane Ackerman. The song "Ooo Baby Baby" as crooned by one Smokey Robinson.

I say all that to say this: I am moved by many things, none of them perfection. None of them haughty or precise or manipulative. None of them professional or studied or "officially sanctioned" in any way. I seldom know what I need until it has arrived. I do know that that shift in my chest, that rock to my world, can come from anywhere—somewhere simple, somewhere complex. Anywhere a moment, a voice, a song, or a poem reaches out and finds someone.

I can assure you that the three winners of this year's Miller Williams series are all—I've checked—mere mortals. Each one took a different road to reach me; each one changed my world in a different way. There is no one voice, and there is no one way to hear a voice.

Let's look at the winners, from third to first, from runners-up to crown, Miss America style.

Red Ocher by Jessica Poli is a lush collision of aubade, cento and ghazal, poems that snug cozily into forms that were born waiting for them, poems that pulse outward from a relentless core of sensuality and heartbreak to embody what nature does to us. I am wholly envious of Jessica, because I find such concise lyricism to be difficult to manage. And having grown up surrounded by concrete and hard edges where pigeons were the only wildlife, I can't help but be mesmerized by a poem like "The Morning After"—

When I opened the door to the coop
and saw three chickens and a mallard lying dead

in the soggy pine chips, I thought the raccoon
had made clean kills of all the birds it wanted

in the night. So forgive me if I shouted
when I walked into the yard and saw the duck

standing motionless, head covered in blood,
a marble statue after a war.

What's stamped on me, what follows me into my dreaming, is the instance after, the necessary sacrifice of the dying duck, who flees, headless, "before it stopped / and sank to the ground where its neck arced / and swung, mourning itself."

What I'm changed by is the breath I hold in from the beginning of the title poem "Red Ocher":

To paint the barn bloody.

After all that planting, the peppers rot off the vine.

Wind was once oil. Soil has memories.

What's lost in the retelling.

To fall apart or believe.

The farmer, filling the wheelbarrow with sawdust, remembering last
year's weather: *That was a different God.*

What the wasp dragging its half-severed tail knows about sorrow.

Jessica teaches a softer violence, the tender face of it. Her deftly crafted stanzas, her mastery of form, her lean uncluttered way of nudging us forward—all those things make *Red Ocher* a book that undeniably deserves the accolades coming its way.

Up next—well hello there, Ms. L. J. Sysko! You are a wildness and a weirdness, and I would like to play a role in unleashing you upon the world. Your book, *The Daughter of Man*, is gleeful and quicksilver, not willing to sit still for categorization. I'm *here* for it.

L. J. is the risk-taker, the unveiler, the irreverent namer of things. Witness "Trompe L'Oeil," a disrespectful ode to a former teacher:

> Like a kid climbing through the window: eyes wide, shirt billowing open with the heat of hijinks, I'm back—grabbing you by the Peter Pan collar to chew gum in your class, drop your hall pass in the toilet, and eat your breakfast for lunch. I won't recover my manners, no, they're pinned up there under the postcards, ribboned fast to a bulletin board between lion and lamb. You sat the girls in the back of the class and taught math to the front. And I guess I have the option of being less mad, but my upset's been tipping on the precipice forever, like a Medici cherub poised for a rotunda-fall.

Let's take a wee tour of L. J.'s mind, shall we? Up next, from the poem "I may":

> If I want, I may ultrasound each month to monitor
> hornets' nest activity. I may bushwhack to witness
> watering-hole power dynamics. If I want, I may
> write ethnographies about cultural reciprocity
> or muse at the wisdom of using blood as currency.
> It's my vagina/uterus/cervix, so you can't tell me
> I haven't wasted whole days microscope-hunched,
> waiting for something to happen.
> Days wishing happenings would stop.

Who can stop there? See more of what I saw:

> **What's stupid**
>
> is, even if aliens do
> mean us harm and descend
> the way they did in comic books—
> all jumbo-almond eyes, peach-pit heads,
> and pistachio-ice-cream skin,
> knocking the totem off Bob's Big Boy roof,
> even if they utter language that's frozen and vegetable,
> even if, with weapons drawn or peace in our puny hearts,
> we're vaporized, liquefied, or harvested as fuel—I'll still feel
> the jubilant force of epiphany. The way a pearl peering out
> of a knife-pried oyster might behold a kitchen.
> The way a woman dwelling within a paneled parlor
> might put the phone receiver down,

return to preparing dinner, folding laundry,
Gunsmoke or *Green Acres*,
having just heard
the unutterable word.

The Daughter of Man is gleefully unapologetic, upending the familiar and blasting it with motion, heat, and consequence. It's a wide-eyed stroll through the real world, reintroducing me to moments I just might remember living—moments made new with liberal dashes of L. J.'s humor and singular insight.

This year's Miller Williams Poetry Prize top choice, *To Be Named Something Else* by Shaina Phenix, absolutely refuses to behave on the page. Something shifted in my chest with the book's very first poem, because I know—actually, was one of—those blue-black summer girls waiting for some bad boys to twist open the fire hydrant and cool us off:

See us,   summered in waters most definitely troubled,   stubborn & never
actually putting any fires out,   rinsing our summertime heavies down into the sewers.
Little Black   so & so's   walk through water   like we Moses or something.
See her, all copper & running over   like she God, a cup,   or something.

With "Hydrant Ode," and with so many of the other poems that make up this electric collection, Shaina enlivens the everyday—the everyday miraculous, the everyday hallelujah, the numbing everyday love, the everyday risk of just being Black and living.

There is absolutely nowhere these poems aren't—we're dancing and sweating through our clothes, terminating a pregnancy in a chilled room of white and silver, finally gettin' those brows threaded and nails did, practicing gettin' the Holy Ghost, sending folks to their rest, having babies, listening carefully to the lessons of elders, and sometimes even talking back.

In the brilliant "La Femme Noire: A Choreopoem," a piece in conversation with Ntozake Shange's *For Colored Girls Who Have Considered Suicide / When the Rainbow Is Enuf*, a young Black girl ("perhaps myself," Shaina suggests) queries the elders in an attempt to pull them closer:

Who are you and whom do you love?

What do you remember about blood?

Who is responsible for the suffering of your mother?

Tell me something you've never said to your body.

Of course, I did what all the fortunate readers of this book will inevitably do. I walked into the poem and answered every question for myself. And with my answers, I found new pathways, new ways to be drawn into Shaina's work.

To Be Named Something Else is a book of reason and reckoning, substance and shadow. It's tender and wide-aloud and just about everything we need right now, when both reason and reckoning are in such woefully short supply. And Shaina's superlative combination of formalism and funk consistently astounds—deftly crafted ghazals, sonnets, the pantoum, the duplex, the sestina, and other usta-be traditional structures (I say "usta-be" because they are hereafter transformed) are all on display here.

And not simply on display. They come to conquer.

Every page is stamped with a defiant signature—in fact, I guarantee there's no way you can flip past "Shug Avery Identifies as Pansexual, Poly, and Dares You to Say Anything about It," "The Burning Haibun Remembers Who I Am," or "American Pantoum with Bullet-Holes & Wall." Shaina Phenix will pull in you, and she will hold you there. And, by God, you won't want to move.

I leave you with a stanza from "Sermon," one that resounds with me, if any one stanza can be said to typify the power of this collection:

> Mother god in the name of Girl—I come to you
> as alive as I know how asking you to be
> an unbloodied knuckle sandwich, be unfucked, and in
> an undulant ocean of selves and salt bone of my befores. Be the first word
> out of my mother's reborn mouth. Be swine-repellent or the pearls that
>   look
> like pearls but don't bust from too much pressing   down. Be that
> which is holy and make dogs deathly allergic. Be
> me in an un-rendable skin-sheet. Let this poem (Earth? Body?) ? Be all
>   of you
> and none of me for the sake of your people.   Amen.

—*Patricia Smith*

ACKNOWLEDGMENTS

Thank you to the following publications and organizations—their editors, judges, and staffs—for publishing individual poems that appear in this collection: *Let Me Say This: A Dolly Parton Poetry Anthology*, Madville Publishing ("The Yassification of Dolly Parton"); *Mississippi Review* ("Landscape with Wisteria"); Robinson Jeffers Tor House Foundation ("M.I.L.F."); *Degenerate Art* ("What a Warrior Whispers" triptych); *Mom Egg Review* ("Everything's Elegy" and "Paula"); *Painted Bride Quarterly* ("Ball Game" and "Relational Identity"); *Missouri Review* "Poem of the Week" ("Pockabook"); *Radar* ("Kristallnacht"); *Moist Poetry Journal* ("Venus & Minerva in Quarantine" and "Fluorescent Mammals"); *SWWIM Every Day* ("I'm undone" and "Trees and paint aren't different,"); *Stirring* ("She wants to be buried in a cocoon,"); *Voicemail Poems* ("Self-Portrait with Bubble Gum"); and *The Pinch* ("Barnegat Light").

For encouragement along the way, thanks also to: Copper Nickel Jake Adam York Prize, Marsh Hawk Press Poetry Prize, Frontier Poetry New Voices Poetry Contest, Mississippi Review Prize, the Missouri Review Jeffrey E. Smith Editors' Prize, Sandy Crimmins National Prize in Poetry, Patricia Dobler Poetry Award, New Millennium Writing Awards 51, Fish Publishing Poetry Prize (twice), the Fourth River Folio Contest, the Pinch Literary Awards, Soundings East Claire Keyes Poetry Prize, Limp Wrist, JToledo5, and Wild & Precious Life Reading Series.

And, my heartfelt gratitude to:

Patricia Smith for making my dreams a book. Your trust in my work, your phone call, the creative freedom you granted me? Honors all. I hope the book makes you proud.

Everybody at the University of Arkansas Press for leading this debut poet through the labyrinth. It is a thrill to be a Miller Williams Poetry Series poet. Thank you.

Artist-collaborators and fellow Delawareans: painter Chloe McEldowney for bringing your extraordinary talents to bear on the cover art. I like to imagine we'd have made Magritte spit out his apple. Thanks also to Kirstie Donohue, photographer, and Tonia Marisa Patterson, makeup artist, for working with me on the cover persona in studio.

K. M. Weiland for treating "Archetypal Character Arcs" on the 2021 episodes of her podcast, *Helping Writers Become Authors*. These caused me to reckon with the heroine's journey, which led to a renovation of my manuscript and a passel of new poems.

Bridget Quinn for her book *Broad Strokes: 15 Women Who Made Art and Made History (in That Order)* (Chronicle Books, 2017)—gifted to me by my daughter Siena Sysko—where I found Artemisia Gentileschi and Paula

Modersohn-Becker, among others, and they got me to thinking about paintings, poem-paintings, and patriarchy.

Virginia Center for the Creative Arts—all of the generous people I met there, both staff members and artists—for the time, space, and fellowship I found on that sunny hilltop twice during the making of this book.

VCCA artist-in-residence Paige Critcher for my "Corn Crib" author photo.

Palm Beach Poetry Festival—coordinators and staff—for honoring me with a 2022 Thomas Lux Scholarship and the gift of a spot in Diane Seuss' workshop.

Diane Seuss for that wonderful, wild week. Thanks also to my fellow Seussian workshoppers.

Maya C. Popa for the 2022 generative workshops just when I thought I was done. Thank you for your clever prompts and splendid facilitation. Thanks also to my fellow Popa workshoppers.

Kim Addonizio for virtual workshops in 2020 and 2021. Thank you for the push to produce during the early days of the pandemic. Thanks also to my fellow Addonizio workshoppers.

Gregory Pardlo for the 2019 Key West Writers' Workshop. Thank you for your incisive questions; they sent me in search of better answers. Thanks also to my fellow Pardlo workshoppers.

Sandra Beasley for the 2018 Delaware Seashore Writers' Retreat jumpstart and the nascent manuscript consultation in 2019. Yours is a fastidiously fine poetic mind; thank you for wielding it graciously on my work. I kept going.

Writerly confidants, friendly distractions, "animals / efflorescent": Anne Marie Macari, Sandra Beasley, Alan Michael Parker, Lee Upton, Ross Gay, Chin-Sun Lee, Julie E. Bloemeke, Dustin Brookshire, Ben Kline, Aaron DeLee, Nan Schiowitz, Mara Raskin, Kathryn Kummer, and Chris Morrow.

Delaware State University President Dr. Tony Allen for my "day job" finding words to match the HBCU movement. Thanks also to Dr. Lynda Murray-Jackson, Dr. Dawn Mosley, my colleagues, and the entire DSU community.

My teachers—all the way through, from Montessori to Pennsbury School District to the Lawrenceville School to Lafayette College to New England College—and former students and fellow teachers at Tower Hill School, where I taught and chaired until 2020. I'm thankful for every minute.

My family: Bob, Jane, and Madeline Jones; Dr. Herbert A. and Lotte Strauss; Dave and Patrice Sysko, and all the extended Syskos.

Finally, MY LOVES: Ryan, Siena, and Reeve Sysko. Poetry's a way of living. You are my life.

THE
MAIDEN

Barnegat Light

In the '80s, my sister—Homecoming Queen
and Prom Queen—with Tawny Kitaen-teased hair
and big boobs, got knocked over by a wave
on this very beach and walked up toward our chairs
unwitting.

Her bandeau top had flipped itself around,
lying on only one breast like a pirate's eye patch,
the good eye commanding all it surveys.
She squeezed her nose then water from her hair,
and the people seated in beach chairs
held their breath, not wanting to tell her
as though the exposure were theirs.

      And they all froze, rapturous of her power:
an Amazon having removed a breast in favor of hunting prowess.

      And they all froze, rapturous of her shame:
Lilith tanned past a Pre-Raphaelite hue save the lone pale fruit.

      And they all froze, vicariously frail:
Eve in the second before epiphany.

      And they all cowered.
A Cyclops, lumbering to a stop
over Odysseus' men, one eye enough
with which to reduce their number
until the sun's glare
and a pointed shaft
put it out.

Pockabook

We made 2nd base out of
oak tree catkins.
       Mound of tumbleweed
       centered.

We made witch's brew out of
a hollow stump.
       Cauldron of acorns
       stirred with twigs.

We made microphones out of
Goody hairbrushes.
       Paddles of glittered plastic
       and shed hair.

We made pockabooks out of
mom's pockabook.
       Pouch of Binaca
       and Jackie O sunglasses.

We made cigarettes out of
candy cigarettes.
       Tuiles of cellulose
       and powdered tapioca.

We made adultness out of
pretense.
       We made it up until
       we believed it. We made

them buy it. We made work fun and
fun work and
       life work and work
       life and work work—

carrying our stirring twigs
like medieval torches,
        brandishing hairbrush microphones
        like ambitious witches, gripping candy cigarettes

like grown women, clutching dusk
like its acquiescence to night owed to our skilled negotiation—.
        Red rover, red rover,
        send her over—

to swim in an estuary
the size of
        our street corner.
        Fish swimming

like loose Velamints—
aspartame-speckled
        in the muddy shoals
        of mom's pockabook—

on its banks, shadows played
our game.
        Feints and steals formed a ceremony
        made up of sisters

and pretense
that time made
        real.

The Mooning 1986 (Etiology of the Cauldron)

Once when my sister and I were roughhousing
with our boy-neighbor, they made fun of me, so
I stood on the guest room bed and mooned them,

pulling my pants down low enough to convey my ire
—all the way to my knees—,
bending over far enough to emphasize

my commitment to the gesture,
—folded in absolute half—.
They laughed harder, a lot harder, doubling and

draped across each other until they lost breath,
and my sister finally wheezed:
We could see everything . . .

. . . I fled the howling room and went to
find my mother, pretending—with my face on fire—
to be interested in the contents of a simmering pot.

She could tell something was amiss, and
when they careened into the kitchen
and told her, she struggled not to laugh,

but soon the whole house closed its eyes,
pursed its lips into a line, and strove
to keep the cackle from boiling over.

Plinko

                              If I held our thermometer up against
a light bulb
              or dipped it in my tea
                        I could stay home
              99.9
100.3
                              & watch *The Price Is Right* at
                                          11 o'clock
                                    from the couch
                        apprentice
                  my mother who narrowed her eyes
            delivered cinnamon toast
              delivered
                        my pillow from upstairs to my
            nest while I
                                          mumbled prices
                                                remarked on groceries I
                        didn't realize were sponsors
                                          watched models ensorcell
                  me gesturing at automobiles like junior hags
                        defeathering jumbo American fowl
                              bee dump da duh
                                    Broyhill dining sets
                              bee dump da duh
                  condensed soup   Tang to the moon
                        tuh dee dee   tuh dee dee   tuh dee dee
                  contestant bounds onstage   spacesuit-boots
                              plants her feet   a flag
                  she comes in with her coffee   stirring slowly
            with a bid   to check my head
            that unabashedly undercuts   *remarks on how warm*
everyone else's bid   *I feel*
      One dollar   *Precisely as warm*
            Too bad   *as tea*
      the actual retail price is   *in that mug*
            Nice try   *Nice try*
                  smile as warm   exactly
                        the temperature of
                        luck
                        dropping

Afterschool Special Rewound

This episode's moral:
never again
eat Doritos prior
       to a night out drinking.

If you throw them up,
they hurt—edges sharp
as a school of
       pencil points returning
       to the blue specter
       where they spawned.

On Formica shores
dotted with fridge magnet
shells, parents wrapped
       us in blankets
       then demanded a
       rational explanation.

We straddled a windowsill,
shimmied a downspout,
jumped a fence,
       and ran from
       a busted party,
       shoving pennies in
              our mouths because we
              heard copper neutralizes
              Breathalyzers.

We've got to match
our stories.

Let's say I'm calling
about math or
Michelangelo.

When you held my hair back . . .
I felt I might dive in,
burst clean onto
      Mad Libs' islands
      of cream-bleached mustaches
      floating like glaring
            mothers at closed, white
            bedroom doors.

Floating doors glaring back
at closed, white mothers.

Hold my eyes open
for contacts,
call in a request,
      dedicate a doorknob
      removed: porthole
      into the sea of Maybe
            I can be
            a Presidential
            Physical Fitness
                  Flexed Arm Hang warrior.

Time my Atari leaps
over oil and water,
around scorpions/
      gold/cobras/fire.

If you leave
the 8th grade dance,
you can't come back in
      and if Victimization
      travels at Shame's rate,
      it will arrive at

Spin-the-Bottle Station—
having departed first
period Language Arts,
    where dots last connected,
    manifesting
    a pastoral
            of pumpkins or kittens.

Training our bras to
train our brains to breathe
shallower like
    the Old Maid double
    bluff—higher isn't
    not better,
            Nothing gold
            can stay though
            1984's
                    sunburn did
                    permanent damage.

We could fake magic,
yanking our will around
Ouija board
    topography,
    but everyone knows
    the loudest
            evangelist's our fraud.

Whoever smelt
it dealt it.

We slept lined up
in sleeping bags
down in basement rec rooms,

stockpiled scratch 'n sniff
stickers inside Trapper
Keepers like
    wartime fatback, folded
    looseleaf dream catchers like
    letters sent to the front,
        popped soda can tabs
        and mounded them:
        epitaphs.

A legion of Brownies
trained to defend
peer pressure's barrage,
      Just say no,
    we repeated like a
    basic training mantra,
        heaved bags of
        microwave popcorn
        against raining flak and
            flood.

We kept virtue frozen
like Thin Mints—hard tack
squirreled away for
    winter's subsistence.

Light dawns black to blue.

Tune in and
take up a position.

Bisected Girl with Vagina

She laid the tampon pamphlet on the bathroom floor,
peering down at its small print and cutaway graphic of
Bisected Girl with Vagina.
Aim for the top of your hiney, her mother said
from out in the hall, mouth pressed to door.
Chin quivering, curled over herself like a
question mark, she said,
It won't go. I can't.
The Voice: *You can. Everyone*
does this. There's nothing special about you.
Then: *Let me in.*
Resolved, she rammed harder.
Muscles ached for days after
and she'd remember
—years later—how
No, the idea of No, I
won't let you in
meant Hurry
and
Harder.

Big Earrings & a Hat

We sat there in health class, middle schoolers pondering

the female reproductive system's shape—
ram's head, elephant ears, O'Keefe with Elvis cape.

The sectional view's an amusement park map.
Rorschach really should've asked this question instead,
for all its exposing truth. Imagine the scene:

boys in one room learning about erection

like crewmen trimming sails,
girls in another rolling

tampon bandages for the infantry.
After battle, birds peck at anything dead,
but they prefer eyes & livers.

In wartime, let's prop our best scarecrows

against their fusillade—
fallopian tube sentries flanking fertile acres.

Pink gingham, big earrings, & a wide straw hat
make a stable nest once flipped,
blown clear of the field.

The Mall

The moon drops one or two feathers into the forest.
        Releases her train of taffeta for us to climb inside.

O, the laughter.
        We're hiding within circular clothing racks—

the moon's waifs, sisters crouching amidst
        whorls of Gloria Vanderbilt and Evan Picone.

Between trees in our silver-branched canopy,
        a dark-haired woman intercedes,

parting leaves, shadows crossing her face,
        she intones into trunk's hollow—

low and tired as though she aspires to
        an Arcadia more lush, far from our valley.

I stand beside her at Cash/Wrap,
        not daring to giggle or move.

Don't tell your father, she says,
        paying half in cash, half credit.

I won't look over at my sister,
        who's scrimmed by a swatch

of hosiery, making faces.
        It is hot to hold a coat.

We trudge past fountains.
        Pennies glint like owls' eyes in the night.

prom

venus was raised in small
rooms with school portraits
descending stairs
pointing to the front door
where she holds
her face   her future
packed like a corsage
in plastic

when she opens the door
her date enters—

hinges creak   satin sweeps
and after she leaves
her little sister holds the light coffin

THE
WARRIOR
(VS. THE
PREDATOR /
PROTECTOR)

Date Rape

Just 16 then, she was laid down
        on a sandy bed and jabbed.

She said, *Hurry up*
        when she meant, May this be over soon.

As when the sun goes behind a cloud.
        She dipped her drunken hand

in sand and fed it into her mouth.
        Grains formed a rune

on her tongue that said, Your life
        won't be yours

unless you and shame collide. She replied
        with nothing like what she meant.

She hoped sleep melted sand.
        The bed, an hourglass, flipped sun

to moon. She thought to say
        enough. Just 16, the boy

jabbing her kept on jabbing
        until she woke again and flew away

like a kid leaping from lifeguard stand
        to sand or a gull dodging a heedless boy.

She rammed louvered closet doors
        off their track. What another boy's

face says when a girl falling
        lands. She spoke not a word

when she washed up
      in a tide coming in and out

of its own accord. She could have asked,
      Did you deliver me? Or

fail to make me drown?
      but when she woke to hands

and a blanket swaddled,
      she thought, There's little difference.

Maybe warn the birds instead.
      This is what they do

when they break your wing
      for you. Trundle you into the car

in a shoebox jabbed with holes,
      pretending it's your decision

to mend. The tide blames the moon.
      Having collided once, too,

she is herself a convalescent.
      Both bruised and bright.

What a Warrior Whispers

After *Self-Portrait as the Allegory of Painting*
(1638–1639), Artemisia Gentileschi

Caravaggio began
      with brush handle dipped in oil,

hushing with silver then
      tracing his route farther

into forest satin,
      dark & loamy as lies.

I   peer   out
      from behind a tree.

A human paintbrush.
      A doe

having drunk
      from her own Red Lake,

shrinking into puddle.
      My virginity went to trial,

where words I'd never spoken
      ringed my fingers then tightened

into gold vises. Their sketch
      mattered more than the girl

I'd drawn.
              On the promontory

of a palette, I stand.
      A sapling   rooted on the edge.

tablescape

hares   pears   plums   pomegranates   women

we're portraiture's chorus line
      having kicked our legs into one

busby berkeley bloom
and opened our necks
to compositions' beheading

    we lie supine   letting light play

    refract   then flee
ermine upstages us

    divans cut us off at the knees
    epistles   pitchers   pearls   win pride of place
unless we moisten lips a little

and part them

       my lamb
one earns this flourish   a daub of lead

white
    applied   heavy
        with a knife

What a Warrior Whispers

After *Judith Beheading Holofernes* (ca. 1620),
Artemisia Gentileschi

Abra, I feathered for us
         a heavy nest with my

grunting cut. Sword & sparrow,
              we bore up our truthful

heft then found our wings
              lacked breadth. We are

Earth-bound forever
              in the same predicament:

oxen with no
              purchase for our yokes.

His dead expression farms
              a familiar furrow:

intention robbed
              of agency. We speak

nothing of chasms
              between what once was

and what could be—
              truth & actuality,

planter & yield,
              soldier &

battlefield, tongues
              mortified on history's

single bed.

Kristallnacht

After "Kristallnacht" occurred in Nazi Germany, female Jews
who did not have "typically Jewish" given names were forced
to add "Sara" to official identification cards.

Sara and
Sara and
Sara and
Lotte
each carry
a crystal
balloon

Sara's rises
floats up high
then hiccups with a
hitch on
a chimney

Sara reads
her tiny
fortune and
sees it crack
so she packs
her trunk
Fragile
and swallows
her future fast

Sara's vanishes
into a cattle car
where thousands of
balloons are herded
and when she goes
to find it in Poland
she never comes back

Lotte makes
hats on the
Lower East Side
using shards
in lieu of
feathers or ribbon

Nothing cuts like
 aftermath except
 a taxi line tether
 from wrist leading back
 to a green hill
 in the distance where heads
 like light bulbs line
 the path
 Sara to Sara to Sara

 and their
 blazing
 vanishing
 point

The Daughter of Man

He's biting that Apple—
snake jaw unhinged, not minding
the slow upstaging meal.

If he commits to suckling
what he damages forever,

he can fancy himself loyal,

mistaking gore for gallantry.
It doesn't occur
that fanging the forbidden

stops him short
of tasting, chewing,

taking her deeper within.

Once we compel him
to free Apple,
with her waxen pallor

and leaf of surrender,
his jaw will ache.

His mouth,

a damp cavern,
will have dripped
its own stalactite fangs solid,

forever propping
his scream

open.

26

Self-Portrait as Molly Pitcher

I wore a Diana Virgin Goddess mask despite my contrary status, pouring pitcher after pitcher for Revolutionary soldiers. O, how I wanted to scrabble over their terrain—rough and uneven—alongside the wagon train, doubling back and over, scouting for the best brook from which to collect, trekking upstream of their latrine, and, with each tipple and ladle into a patriot mouth smoked and pursed, I lost a little of my name. *Over here* morphed from a whistle into *Pitcher* then someone added *Molly*, and I guess I could've put the bucket down, subordinated myself a little less like a spaniel than a swatch of fodder for the cannon, but at the time, they seemed basically the same. *Betsy Ross, you know her?* As though hookers working the same corner are necessarily friends? I never met her until they locked us both up in an inset box. There in the basement of a history textbook page, we didn't even speak. My role was only pathetic volunteer, keeping parched heroes hydrated, but Betsy, she stitched and sewed their symbols together. After that, all we saw were stars.

The Daughter of Man

He's chased me around a clock face
with his Uncle Sam finger

foreshortened between my crossed eyes.
Once the woolen itch from his hat
pays dividends, he'll evangelize

membership in the monolith.

Magritte gave him an apple.
I'd give him a vagina—

the ones nobody draws
on study hall tables because
they're obsessed with penises instead—

and he can talk through it,

letting it filter his excuses
until he marvels

at its self-cleaning efficiency.
Unlike a mouth,
which is a dirty thing.

Luck or Something Other

The day I was rescued from Not Drowning
by a Long Beach Island lifeguard
          he crashed into the surf & grabbed me.

I thrashed away because   objectively
          I had been swimming   seized now
          accosted by a blonde   tan   teenaged

demigod. I was only 14 & wearing
my Practice Speedo for serious
bodysurfing even though my mom preferred

me in a bikini. She'd say   *Flaunt it*
while you can   aim for separation from the pack
          from his grasp   which he tightened instead

          a vise squeezing me breathless about the
ribs   lifting me bodily like a reeling marlin.
I fought harder & yelled things like

Stop!   I don't need saving!
I'm not drowning! His grip grew hysterical & my mother
          in her cover-up   despising

of getting wet   came just so far to tideline
          offered lukewarm rebuttal
          winked at me for becoming

A Helpless Spectacle   for staging a precocious pick-up.
Like a cat that mid-bite grows enamored
of its own jaw's force   the lifeguard

doubled his grip   growling   *I got you!*
My whole body roiled with alarm. All This for
swimming   swimming I thought

        at least I imagined that's what I had been
doing   but I must've seemed somehow
Other.

She's a competitive swimmer   Mom intoned
      very fast   as we jounced clear
up the beach to dune grass where he

put me down. There I transformed
for them   a Monster
      begrudging   boiled red   ungrateful

      embarrassed   winded   a haul
deposited
beneath the lifeguard's panting valor

My mother snapped a picture
of us together then one
of just me   spent

arriving back
into my own
account.

The Daughter of Man

Apple presents only one side,

deploys makeup's chiaroscuro
to bronze what's bruised,

but I've entered the Garden
with supplies to stanch
her sucking wound.

I've got a tampon in my bag

to stick up his nose where Apple's
struggle bloodied it and I'm

closing his mouth,
grabbing his shoulders,
and turning him around

to show him the ocean.

I'm here to triage Apple,
suture her gashes, daub

her cider tears,
and wipe paint
from canvas until

she can see herself.

Self-Portrait with Bubble Gum

My hoodie's grey with varsity
block-letter appliqué:

B A S I C

no need to look too long
because my hair's brown and
cut medium-length neither
straight nor curly and I'm
average by any actuarial
measure I'm banal danger in a
full face of makeup I'm half a
sour citrus dolloped
with cottage cheese and
maraschino-topped Sweet 'n
Low strapped in sidecar I'm
Unlimited Salad Bar who
accompanied its mother to
Aerobics   I'm a serrated
grapefruit spoon when all you
want are Lucky Charms I'm
end-of-week TV Guide used
as a coaster because Nat'l
Geographic's got eyes I'm an
'80s album cover rendered
animate ponytail Ray-Bans
pink Hubba Bubba blown into
face-obscuring bubble lips
pursed into an
                    O
of Greek choral epiphanic
echo
zombie   cheerleader
grimacing at pyramid's base
mouthing *Please   no*

What a Warrior Whispers

> After *Susanna and the Elders* (1610),
> Artemisia Gentileschi

Men I once knew skulk in cloaks
       at horizon line:

archers' clouts I pierce
       for practice. This wall's

replete with What I've Been
       hunting so far—

hare   &   hart
       set Ready Up under

short-order lamps.
       They offer themselves

to *Diana's Arbalest*,
       like truckers stopping

at my dangerous diner,
       sign blinking neon in the night,

while I, a sharpened shaft—
       Heart Attack on Rack,

Blonde with Sand, Mystery
       in the Alley—

permit myself
       to let fly.

Order's up,
       Cherry.

The Yassification of Dolly Parton

Even from behind a counter
under a caul of flaming hair
Jolene must've seen how a harrier carries her call

tree to mountain   hoists whole the holler
teasing it high   or how heaven

loans a magpie one single sequin at a time

how a warbler whistles beside snow-melt slide
until her heart   a hunter
wheels in exercise   how a hawk

casts her shadow   behind peacock disguise
Oh   little mouse   listen—

you're from Barefoot Rise   below Rib-Thin

hunkered under a tinsel umbrella
humming the tune   of spangled sky
gamboling brookside   A steel on silver strings

you tremble   Spread wide   wings sound
loud as the first time

you heard there was such a thing as song

Let her lift
your longing   pretty
until you forget you

alone can't float   flee   fly
Dolly!

Dive!   Swipe want from a meadow   pince its warm hide

Roll   peck   break   blind
This bank where desire mole-holes to survive
            Hold   It   Up

Write a note then push it   reaaaal   slowww
acrylics scraping through

a window in time

Here   *beautiful*
                                RUN

                                                my lines

Paula

After Self-Portrait on Her 6th Wedding
Anniversary (1906), Paula Modersohn-Becker

Cutlery plinks,
silver tinks

in brothels
busy behind

the lines.
Bodies lie

crowned by
dragonflies. Apricot

trees blown
to matchwood

preside acres-wide
like nursery

wallpaper flocked.
She loses

count of
craters—maize

valley pitted,
pounded. Dogs

and cats
come skulking

back like
sense that

vanished returning
en masse.

Here's lull
enough within

for taking
stock. Roots,

men, blood,
and claws

dig in.
Picking their

way, horse
and rider

canter across
piebald ground—

that fertile
spell cast

like a
die between

wars thrown
by mothers.

THE

QUEEN

Did anybody ask

Odysseus, *Where've you been?*
19 years' passage filled to
wine goblet rim & over,
spilling into banquet hall tales
for weeks post-return/post-slaughter.
Rapt assembly listened then
by turns—uproarious laughter.
Somebody came running with egg
tempura in hand, tiles of mosaic
on a platter: *Sir! Sir! We must*
beg of you to tender for us
an angle of repose while you
weave like no other
the story of your absence.

It's too much to imagine he'd
have demurred & said,
Just one. My wife was swallowed whole
by the whale to whom she'd
given swim lessons; my wife
stood sentry at the transom of a door
hashmarked with the growth
of Alone; my wife took neither lover nor
foe, meeting all in Gray Middle;
my wife lived, commanded, raised
our son up to Taller as I debauched,
debased, & marauded, losing
thousands of lives save my own;
if love exists, it dwells in restraint,
in the song, the pattern sewn into the whale's
ribs from within. Some say the book
about mothers' love's been written.
My men, my men, I say again, I am No
Man if I don't at least read the one

she would've done
had she not—just this morning
as we all sat here drinking & carrying on—
stripped herself naked & gone
for a motherfucking swim.

A woman did not write

the myth of Sisyphus,
which entails a guy pushing a boulder
uphill forever. For a more apt
objective correlative,
one must look no further than
a newborn's mother.
There, the colicky rock
rolls much louder
and she cries when it
latches on for dear life.
Then the rock grows up
and starts the whole thing over.

Relational Identity

The car salesman tells me about safety,
quipping, *After all, we're just bags of water,*
and I have to steady myself because
he got me. That's the line. That's what'll do it—
glib characterization of mortality makes me
hot, and even though he's not attractive,
to my eye, I'm imagining reclining with him
beneath the moonroof and testing the limits
of this award-winning safety cage.

I'm exaggerating, of course, as I'm wont to do,
but there's a thin scrim between us and
infinity anyway so why not mistake the gas and
brake occasionally? See what a little adrenaline does
for the hairdo, Like a '50s-style coiffure
mussed after clandestine sex.
What's more hubristic than a beehive?
A touch croissanty in the mid-section—
cantilevered, lacquered layers, the acme of
mid-century post-industrial misogyny?
That woman's going nowhere fast.

I love this absurd life, how irony blinks
when I change lanes, warning me
despite necessity's manifest agenda
that I keep going. *DANGER!*
my nervous system shrieks,
and I've stopped hushing it
with antidepressants and such because
I couldn't even feel the steering wheel—
too amenable to turn my head and
check mirrors. I'd just put it in Reverse
and hope for the best.

There's an in-between, and what's printed
on my license proves it.
Says here: I'm me,
living in this place, looking like this,
now. So, I don't really need
absolute calm to see clearly or
the wife and mother roles listed
to verify my import though they are
flagship features.

One bag of water to another—
I pour some into them, they pour into me,
and we share the way the weather cycle looked
in 7th grade when I learned it between units on
geology and trees. I knew those cloud formations cold
and how mica glinted, the way a geode formed,
and that female ginkgos smell
when they shed their leaves and berries.
That's how we know it's fall.

What's stupid

is, even if aliens do
mean us harm and descend
the way they did in comic books—
all jumbo-almond eyes, peach-pit heads,
and pistachio-ice-cream skin,
knocking the totem off Bob's Big Boy roof,
even if they utter language that's frozen and vegetable,
even if, with weapons drawn or peace in our puny hearts,
we're vaporized, liquefied, or harvested as fuel—I'll still feel
the jubilant force of epiphany. The way a pearl peering out
of a knife-pried oyster might behold a kitchen.
The way a woman dwelling within a paneled parlor
might put the phone receiver down,
return to preparing dinner, folding laundry,
Gunsmoke or *Green Acres*,
having just heard
the unutterable word.

Trees and paint aren't different,

Pollock might've said when he splattered summer's last shiver—satisfied, sweating, searching for his Pabst Blue Ribbon among his cans arrayed in the garage before beer pong's rush was amplified by *Smells Like Teen Spirit* and we parked our Ten Speeds for good and then an English teacher said *Nothing's as it seems* about *Macbeth*, about men becoming forest and forest becoming men and birth wasn't quite being born and that's when the first sledgehammer struck, when This and That crashed together, when a wall meant less than its damage, when negative space solidified and we got used to its bitterness like what's burnt on a marshmallow or Jägermeister's licorice grimace. Now we're older, now we're mom—the same age now as she was the summer we begged for a treehouse. *Let's make a fort* under the willow tree instead, carrying loads back and forth—In to Out and back again after roller skating in the basement, listening to records: Donna Summer *Toot toot hey beep beep* or Stevie Nicks *Just like the white winged dove Sings a song Sounds like she's singing Who baby who* perched on a dark limb with space between for us to twirl—*You go first* around the lally column around the willow's trunk around the treehouse we never built but we imagined would've felt like floating on a raft borne by a cloud or winging like an owl among the boughs gliding through our canopy's fractals to circle circle circle our tree with invisible thread like spun sugar thrown by a baker sloughing rain like paint cast benevolently from above with a can in hand and from that vantage point flying likely looks the same as September's first leaf signing the wind's name

I once had a history teacher

whose walls were ribboned with a timeline—

from one treaty

to war to treaty to war

with civilizations' rising,

falling held firmly in line.

It bothered me

I'd never heard of most of them before

as though understanding

ought to come species-encoded.

We made board games with trade routes,

disease cards, and blight tokens.

The advent of fire and iron

precipitated good fortune

or demise every time,

but I loved the laminated surface—

rectilinear order

where misfortune and boon

were statistically predictable—

and our group advanced quickly

from prehistoric to Bronze.

Surprise attack

from another 6th grade section

did us in, but it was an epic upset

that should never have happened.

Our system of religion was matriarchal

and ecologically rooted, our republic

fair and green.

For years, Mr. Snyder displayed

our game

on his Windowsill of Fame.

Empire of Fire

With bindle packed and on her back,
an affronted soul walks away
from home to sit on the curb—

blind with rectitude and blue
with fury until she's tired
of sitting there without

a route or ride. I did that once
as a little kid: ran away,
making it two corners past

our schoolbus stop before I
sat. I'm sure my mom could see me
from a window, but she waited,

testing my will. When night fell,
our neighborhood had bats that swooped
black against twilight's Magritte blue.

I knew it was time to go back
because home felt better from
that distance, if implausible

with its lights shining golden yellow.
Now, I'm meant to test my own
mettle: thanking goodness for slow,

tearful walks around the block,
feeling grief set me down
on the curb awhile amidst bats

that buzz almost comically close.
Maybe they swoop (circling to drop
parentheses around what's over

and done, embracing it in
gathered air), or, more simply,
to loop closer for a look

at a fellow mammal so big
yet otherwise broken down.
Earthbound.

At blue hour's end, when I return,
walking up the driveway again,
how warm my lamps look from outside.

Like I've built an empire of fire.

scherenschnitte

In memory of my grandmother,
Lotte Strauss (1913–2020)

she's cut from
absence
that breathes
behind her
shape
little limbs/
lonely hem
defined
by evergreen
boughs holding
her hands
snowflake flat/blowing
her pigtail braids
out like a wish
first one
braid espaliers
around a lake/
over a meadow
the other
a little
strained
trains back
pointing like a
crossroads finger
at paper's
border
where no one's left
but her figure
tearing against
the mat
black like soil
against buried silver

Everything's Elegy

Swallowed—winging my goggle eyes around inside Jupiter's tyranny—
I feel like Metis or her daughter: Minerva—in birth throes,
delivering myself from skull-thick cruelty.

I've been crying a lot lately, in traffic
while driving from grocery to home and vice versa.
On occasion, I arrive at optimism:
press the sunroof button, goddess divine, and rise
like a middle finger into the weather!
Let whatever pathetic fallacy brews outside be thine!
On other occasions, I am:

Ismene—left-lane-proceeding, mumbling in retrospective rehearsal.
Shoulda said this, shoulda said that, or:
Cordelia—cast in road trip movie,
gripping the steering wheel within a skeletal chassis,
pantomiming freedom on a lurching gimbal.

And to protag is different from what anyone supposed, and weepier.

I've been crying facing people whose business isn't mine.
Choices are few and actually binary: to mute awkwardly,
let storm clouds amass on my face's green-screen map,
or speak anyway and into the wind
like a hurricane correspondent, gales lashing my cheeks
and whipping my hair, one lightning flash burnishing another

until I remember I'm neither meteorological nor mythological,
just a person whose hope outpaces reality
no matter how fast she guns it off the lights
or how many groceries spill and roll around the back:
daredevil pickles packed in glass perching with eggs on the precipice.

My optometrist asked, *this lens or this one?*
This one/this one? How about now?

Until the entire proposition dissolved
into equal parts panacea and failure. I cried,
but he mistook my apoplexy for dilation.
I kept daubing with my fisted tissue, squinting into the blur
beneath a gargantuan E
spread as if pinned on an entomologist's board.

A common housefly,
Metis had 3,000 simple eyes mounted together
at the front of her body—figureheads on the ship of
Futile Vigilance.
There's no "ship name"
for Jupiter and Metis, for what a hack
without compunction will do to a Titan,
let alone a myth

Up Route 202 and back again,
I pass a woman I used to know—
her car coming, mine going—
and though she doesn't see me, I see her:

a bust above the dash, shining like marble in a museum rotunda.

I'm undone

they declare—
Regency heroines in climactic throes,
Victorian fainters, Romantic lovers—
in command of an iamb
even as they succumb to forces
greater than will alone. I'm undone,
we each announced this year
and last year and especially the year
that rent childhood's seams for us.
You know the one. That did it.

Mine rises like a peony above a long fence—
heavy, layered with petals like organdy over satin over
petticoats and hosiery, enshrouding what's underneath—
the done of undone
pulsing within memory,
breathing quietly, sipping from a narrow straw.
My peony survives because tiny ants
tend to her day and night like footmen
in foretelling livery.

Every spring, I bring my peony inside
and hold her head underwater
to drown the ants. Ritual
becomes her.

15 Minutes

I am Apple Compote
to your Salisbury Steak,

tin foil hearts
adjacent for frozen

life. Waltz with me,
my boxy beloved—bound

& buoy from one
deep depression to

the next, Armstrong-leaping,
frolicking, connected. Michael Jackson's

sequined glove carried
a torch for

his feet, Kirk Gibson's
bum knee held out

long enough to
do his own

elbows a favor—pumping
him around 2nd, 3rd

for the prodigal
return, knees grimacing:

*I hope you're enjoying
this,* this time, this

Very Special Episode—
even though they

never met. Here, on
a windless path, can

we double back
to when we

each clicked a channel
& the other, the other?

We'll convert our
film, Beta, & VHS,

to vivid color—
rising, falling, awhirl—

holding home in the
window, inside our irises

like a jettisoned
rocket to Remember.

When I recount my
dream to you later,

I'll murmur: On
a powder moon,

we danced, held hands,
held frame through layers,

but how we
bounded nowhere special

was so familiar until
I awoke from my

separate slumber to
wonder whether I

still followed your lead
as though on a

shiny tether. Served
backward into the

void via teaspoon's measure.

She wants to be buried in a cocoon,

her decomposing corpse becoming food for a planted tree.
This presumes a lot on behalf of the tree. But, she's in
excellent condition so, as a meal, she'd be more organic than most,
what with yoga, Pilates, undyed hair, & the diet requiring
she pour melted butter churned from Irish grass-fed cows' milk into
her morning coffee. Whether it's Elm or Linden, Hickory or Tulip,
these are her choices, like men on Tinder. Tulips are the tallest
Eastern hardwood & Hickory's the broad-shouldered one
often seen standing in a field all alone. Whichever she chooses,
her tree will embrace her bundle—fetal position & upside down—
mixing her into a batter, a paste, muesli thinned with rainwater.
When he lifts the pabulum to his lips, he'll sip & she'll rise, climbing
higher, stripping herself bare, leaving clothes on the stairs, laughing so
only he can hear. Rings mark the years.

What's stupid

is driving a car with an epitaph decal stuck to the back window.
What can you see except grief spelled backwards in rearview?
At traffic lights, I decipher your exhaust plume rune—
middle initial, nickname, life span—
and self-recriminate for trying to deduce how death came
because this tombstone wasn't my idea, it was yours,
and while you tune your radio,
I'm standing graveside instead of you,
facing this thing down with your beloved, calculating
whether it's better to wave our arms,
make ourselves look big, run,
scream, serpentine, climb a tree.
Or close our eyes, having done the math,
and sing.

THE

MAVEN

M.I.L.F.

The M's self-explanatory.
The I
        is a boy-man's first-person perspective—
a set of eyes evaluating
her body's sensual potential
        relative to his anticipated pleasure:
a furtive cost-benefit analysis
taking into account hidden value against
        asset depreciation.

L stands for like, but it's the K in like
that I like for its indecorous clack
        of tongue against soft palate
followed by a tiny capitulating exhale—
breath that subordinates itself
        to the future's pulsing throb,

a throb I can feel from here
as I stand at the gas pump
        near a boy-man topping off
his already-full tank
with aggressive lever-pumps.
        He's like a nearly satiated baby
nodding off to sleep
but awakening with a start
        once the nipple pops free of his lips.
He's got a clamping latch
and loud, complaining colic.

That cry's going to shatter your nerves,
the nurse said to me postpartum,
        and my firstborn—my daughter—did,

but I got my nerves back.
Or, we grew them anew
       together.

My favorite nerve's still the one
connecting my nipple to
       my contracting womb.
I'd never have known
how animal and wild I am
       but for that burning flare,
casting light enough
by which to survey the ground
       of my body's farthest biomes.
Boy-man at the gas station
doesn't know nipples, or nerves, or
       wombs from Adam, but
judging from his handling of this moment,
he knows what the F signifies.
       His thoughts' transit
from M to F
seems quick,
       prematurely coming
without verification
of my M status
       or the length, depth, or
breadth of his own L.
What I think
       he knows best is
I.
He's an I expert,
       giving tours of local,
erect monuments to: being.

And his being wants me to know
he sees me: being.
       I to I.
And for that, I thank him.
His is an affirmation
       of a kind, here at Pump #3.
Even as his gaze travels
across my body, he's tearing the receipt
       hard and fast away from the pump,
crumpling it in a clenched fist as
his eyes move like the jet stream that
       rakes then dips
across America's
breadbasket, dropping heat
       and moisture down and down,
before rising up and
peeling out
       to sea.
In a Ford F-150.

Moist Self-Portrait

I'm ovulating so everyone looks better to me today
than they did yesterday. It's as though June moved
into my quiet rooms & now our cycles coincide like
girlfriends or sisters whose swollen sunlit
afternoons discharge into rain unremitting. Sky as
colander, strawberries loaded in for a soaking rinse,
I pulse—a rainspout panting, a woman aware this
weather won't last. Today, however, I drip in time
with my own seedy red heart.

To the hypothetical hostile man in the audience:

Thank you for standing up & grappling with the open mic
like it's your dick turned rapacious cobra   I guess we'll all
watch you charm it back into its deplorable little basket

Thank you for dumping misogyny's contents
like a pirate's treasure chest carried in for queen's review
        at my feet   at my throat   where you aspire
to see decadent ostentation like your worldview worn

Such booty, such jewels—patently compensatory
        heavier than is practical in summer & I can't
wear them all because they clash with the semiotics
of my outfit   garishly contrast with my values   &
I'd honestly stagger under the weight   too bowlegged to stand

or move without aid   but I think that's likely what you desire
        to hobble me   you swashbuckler bereft of boat
        of map   of guiding star   other than an audience
captive   borrowed like an archipelago of sugar   Quick!
    you think   before they dissolve out of hearing
forever   I see you   I got you   I know from whence

your fountain of youthful resentment flows   but I am not
the unwitting galleon or biddable pretender you imagine though
my cannons may impress & I was taught to speak fluently the language
of my oppressor   Please gather your wits
your snake   your chest   don a pair
of binoculars & see
        we're out here sailing on the same ocean where

I'm plainly not to blame for the doldrums you're in
        You   like me
do not lack
for wind

Trompe L'Oeil

Like a kid climbing through the window: eyes wide, shirt billowing open with the heat of hijinks, I'm back—grabbing you by the Peter Pan collar to chew gum in your class, drop your hall pass in the toilet, and eat your breakfast for lunch. I won't recover my manners, no, they're pinned up there under the postcards, ribboned fast to a bulletin board between lion and lamb. You sat the girls in the back of the class and taught math to the front. And I guess I have the option of being less mad, but my upset's been tipping on the precipice forever, like a Medici cherub poised for a rotunda-fall.

Mrs. K., you taught me that certain things weren't mine to have.

Mrs. K., you taught me not to ask.

Mrs. K., you taught me to accept confusion.

You taught me to pretend the door to your teacher's coat closet was a portal to a much larger room because we sat—dutiful and diligent 2nd graders, the way you admonished us to be—while you went inside with the janitor and disappeared. We never asked even though all thirty of us knew its phone booth dimensions: big enough for one coat and a broom—and, apparently, two full-grown adults. And when you came out—three connect-the-dot run-offs later—I'd like to recall you tugging your pearls and taming flyaways with nervous hands, but I think not. I see you clearly: circulating among rows one through four, calmly cooing and crooning. Like pedestrians quizzical about an airbrushed crater, the girls blinked and tried to puzzle perspective out.

I'm untying this blue satin ribbon and freeing our violin from effigy. I'm translating *This is not a pipe* for those who don't already know. I'm walking to the front of Room 2B, past those kids still sitting there in 1982, past me in corduroy culottes, past the guinea pig in its box, past the closet door where you found love's semblance.

To your desk. But I'm not going to sit. I'll stand. Mrs. K, I'll wait. I'll hold up my fingers 1-2-3. Do you see it? The picture I've painted for you . . .

. . . of my thanks.

I may

kick my proto-coniferous tree stump,
       let it topple onto its side and watch life teem
through its warp and weft, centipedes trilling
       chords across its soft strings, if I want.
I may warm my hands above its combustion,
       hold conference with fire, or feed calendars into flames
if I want. I may measure every drip of iceberg melt,
       float atop its last cube like
a polar bear cake topper to doom if I want.
       If I want, I may ultrasound each month to monitor
hornets' nest activity. I may bushwhack to witness
       watering-hole power dynamics. If I want, I may
write ethnographies about cultural reciprocity
       or muse at the wisdom of using blood as currency.
It's my vagina/uterus/cervix, so you can't tell me
       I haven't wasted whole days microscope-hunched,
waiting for something to happen.
       Days wishing happenings would stop.
With a will of its own, a confidence supreme,
       ineffable animal authority,
if she does at all,
       she will smile
when she's good and ready.
       We are scientist and subject,
and our experimental outcome:
       oh, we want.

Landscape with Wisteria

Purple, dangling
from an arbor,
crowned with buzzing bees—
      breathtaking freedom
      and unabashed being.
      It is difficult to believe
          such liberty
          grows from the ground.

This pageant
draws the eye for
a half mile and walkers
      stop and point,
      wishing they had
      an arbor such as this
          under which to sit
          with beverages
          and a friend or three,
              but it needs bracing
              at the root
              since it pulls itself up
                  out of the soil
                  and strangles its trusses,
                  enacting irony
                      in a way someone like
                      Newton or Einstein
                      would have understood.

I've been warned
not to plant wisteria
by those familiar with
      its self-destructive
      habit.
      I understand

and empathize with
both vine and cynic.

In high school,
a young, feminist
English teacher
        pointed out
        how little
        physical space
                women occupy
                relative to men.
                I found this truth
                        so salient
                        that I trained my posture
                        to expand, self-consciously
                                standing
                                like Colossus
                                for a while.

What gravity holds down
may protest—spitting up
cold soil
        like a baby
        who is really
        just an elaborate
                gastrointestinal tract
                at the beginning—
                guts with a voice box
                        that can cry out but
                        lack language to tell us
                        This really hurts or
                                Please send me back.

Being new to this Earth,
babies settle for
curling fingers
     around ours
     or scraping their own
     tender faces with
          sharp fingernail edges,
          not knowing yet,
          of course, as we do,
               that they,
               themselves,
               are pain's cause,
                    that their hand belongs to
                    their brain
                    and will take commands
                         in due time, as long as
                         greater forces permit.
                         There will be paper hats
                             shaped like cones
                             for such occasions
                             and numbers tied
                                  to the mailbox, riding
                                  the wind.

As long as blooms
attend the party
in fragrant, fruitless pursuit
     of heaven,
     it will have been
     worth it.
          And bees
          show up wearing
          gold knee-socks
               knit of future flowers.

I will have more
of this even if
I have to build
        something sturdier
        for it to ruin.

Pool

As I sit on a lounger in yellow-pink September,
I look up to see a monarch sailing about
against a sky I can only honestly describe
as azure. Here's a cerulean pool cut like
a quilt panel into the lawn, which is genuinely
emerald, and for an added touch, some wag
has left a gigantic sliced lemon floating
and scudding against the pool's walls
with a gentle breeze. The monarch seems
to follow the lemon as though they're tethered.
I lie back and think about my gorgeous luck
to be here—alive, well-fed, safe, able, cognizant,
and so on—until I get greedy then wonder
how much better this moment would be if
you were here, if we were together. And,
of course, this brings me to—
as the butterfly dips behind a tree in shadow
(and so it, too, must know)—
how difficult it was to please my mother.

Trauma Theory

There's no getting around it,
whatever callous or barnacle you're hiding
      under your thumb.

Even if it's a wart
you got from a smiting amphibian,
      it's not your fault.

You didn't ask for it
to hunker & settle
      uninvited.

You were just walking from A to B—
locker room to pool deck, say, or
      forest to field—

when it happened. Your route once took you
by some Black Angus cows & the bull
      let you pass though

he moved not an inch other than
to take a stupendous whiz
      & you laughed.

Here's your autumn walk, poet.
Here's a wordless encounter
      for you to freight

with metaphorical gravity. But, no,
they were cows & you were you.
      Contemporaries

breathing—chewing in one case &
listening to music in the other.
      What you seek

to avoid may choose to leap into your path
& become predatory. But, likely as not, not.
        There ought to be

data. (This is the case to be made for math.)
As a child, your father told you:
        That animal

is more afraid of you than you are of him. And,
other than, well, times without number,
        that wisdom's borne

fruit. What to do about the lasting kiss of loss?
About grief that hunts you, host? No matter
        how you freeze it,

burn it, ignore it, or starve it of sunlight,
back it grows. Choices do not abound.
        Pin it down

with your thumb, twisting your fingers
painfully around . . . or wear it like
        a signet ring,

crested with its tiny coat of arms—
a caldera long-ago cooled,
        perched high upon

your writing hand. From above,
survey your realm & marvel
        at the odds.

High Time

Time lapses blue to blue
        with bees pulling day's
gold lamé curtain

wide. Such excess—
        our spinning. Earth's a
fragrant, peachy thing, whirling

out of hand & juice runneth
        over into volcano
revolution. We live

on the surface where
        scratch 'n sniff plumes
atomize peach perfume & breath

depends upon our
        founding stone's premise.
In the beginning,

someone screamed
        an orgasmic shout &
we turned to witness

Desire dawn. The sun's souvenir
        was bitten.
Let's fumble together

toward the Bacchanal,
        feast & crawl as ants
on a cupcake. Let's heft

our share of frosting until
        labor begets new Hunger—
cycling around—, or

forgetting our charge,
        we lick ourselves sick.
Call me yours, lover,

since we're here
        circling the same spot.
Declare me *Your Rock*

in hard times, but
        remember
a rock is a mount

from which to
        pontificate &,
sure, it's high time

for espousing.
        A rock is
a diving board

from whence to jump
        &, yes, there's plenty
of water rising.

A rock isn't Love
        but Earth holding
its breath blue.

The stone has its reason,
        flesh knows none.
Hold me how a tree

holds

its

fruit.

Like Poetry

Can people who hate poetry stop saying,
when they see, for example, a splendid basketball dunk,
     It was like poetry?

Can people who flee from a poem—
     panting, necks craning,
     eyes crossing as one Kong-lumbers near &
     eclipses their sun—just   enjoy the shade?

Can people who, when a poet declares what they do
because somebody asked,   *And what do you do?*
upon hearing the answer
     not shrug cavalierly, mutter excuses, and grin
     into their gin?

The poet stands there, accustomed
to hailing from a neighborhood
     no one wishes to visit, yet everyone acts like
     they deliver its mail.

     Omg, that pleather poncho's like poetry!
     That orangutan spit-take TikTok! Like, poetry . . . I mean like . . .
     Tee shot, sand wedge, rim out— Total. Poetry.
     Samosa! . . . sectional sofa! . . . skeeball score! . . .
     shuttlecock! . . .

Everything's poetry but poetry.

Can we, people, cross over onto Poetry's neat streets,
laid out with warm welcome in mind, where
real estate's scaled for human-sized
animals & their pet people to reside?

     Bring your nails, hair, softshell crab,
     bong, melatonin, dildo,
     pumpkin-popcorn-kumquat latte,

gumbo, brunch buffet, & sorbet
to cleanse your palates.

I've seen what happens when we bring poems
out of our shining kitchen and plunk them down like pie,
like portents,   like Unapologies on a plate—
white plate   clean cloth   blank face—   and say,
Try it. You'll like it. And the forkful—
fluorescent & bursting with fruit & fat & power
espouses a line, its favorite line, on the way to
oblivion.

Dull roots stir, soaking it in—such flavor. Inside—
      inside! a world having
      moved with magic & saliva   nerves & nothing,
      now gone forever, but . . .
      Oh! It was there. It spoke,
      painted music piquant   scrawled words   *Umami*
      mine   whispered
      Sugar   *you've arrived*
      you're   alive.   I
      heard   saw   swallowed   yearned
      for a mulligan   I
      was more me   than
      me for   once
      edified   open-eyed
      new   never   again
      I swear

      Poetry

      let

      me

      be

Surface Tension

I like the beach when everyone else leaves.
        When we sit on the lip high tide's creating—

the ocean a bowl lifted & on offer.
        We're cantilevered on the elbow-edge

of Earth's round table: two terrestrials
        discussing how likeable our kids seem

or ways we'd spend a Powerball jackpot.
        We'll leave here in a few days & fly back

to Philly where things are sepia & colder.
        Oz to Kansas/Bright to Brown/Glenda to Gulch.

On the beach, we're alone in Technicolor:
        after lifeguards split & sandpipers return

to rove for supper. If I lean forward,
        I feel I could sip from Atlantic's rim,

arranging myself like a supplicant
        or animal, bending my neck down

until my lips meet Sea Green thinning to
        Apricot in slanted sun before

soaking-in Silver. If we could lap
        the oceans—humans drinking, slaking thirst

at will—we'd have drunk them dry by now &
        formed political factions founded on

whose sips over-sipped or prejudices
        based on shades of human lips. People kneel

to kiss the ground when they land, having flown
        in a machine we invented for the purpose.

I'd rather kiss the sky or sea. Drop
        my pebble in reverence to difference

& forget how hard Earth's pulling us down.
        I'd rather point out our position

on this ledge—how it tricks the eye—,
        hold your hand & tell you a story

I've never told of the diorama
        I made in 4th grade: a triceratops,

formed from clay complete with Elizabethan ruff
        —fringe that tipped like petals

of a fierce flower—, dinosaur lips pursed
        to a tin foil & rubber cement puddle.

She was ginger in her thirst, even dainty
        despite the defensive armor,

unaware of her blind spots or
        the asteroid's fireball crayoned in

Sunset Orange, bearing down
        from the shoebox's upper corner.

THE
CRONE

Pleasure in the Age of Overwhelm

My right hand is charged with redemption of the Now.
It will ache later. Lightning flashes
on loamy banks beside my clitoris. What else is there
this Afternoon when I'm meant to read   write
          attend the tragic pageant of the news? Generations have
abdicated. In the Age of Overwhelm   may as well be honest.
In our separate provinces   humans pretend to work
from home   but we're all scrolling doom
then palpating the ache   massaging our plight a little
then rhythmically keeping time
on muffled timpani beneath fleece throws.

Such a rite   our thunder:
Nature is never finished.
For each wrath-wrought bolt wreaking down
          our benevolence can still tender rain across
the fruited plain   plump clouds in
spacious skies   swell waves of amber grain.
Come! I beg you   listen to the hush just after
crisis. All is soaked and sated   bright with
shameful excess. How do we explain? I've
turned cartoon
and you: caricature.

I'm just reading.
I'm watching a show. I'm
finishing a document.
I'm gonna loll and lie
here a while. Are you headed out?

Once the car backs down the driveway   we beat
hasty retreat to the couch and love
ourselves for old times' honor.
A lesser God groans
          just relieved
to feel   at all   alone.

Venus & Minerva in Quarantine

Beauty's feeling fugitive
       furtive & sallow
in her bathrobe
       standing ragged
at the fridge

Wisdom peers in
       like an owl perched
on a midnight limb—
       once she was Madame X in her dark dress
vamp with a raptor's eye
       aloof to
matters mundane as
       dinner until
they slithered
       suggestively
by—

Now silence strings itself
       on a necklace
between them
       as fragile as life

Calendar pages
       fold into pearls
hoping to surf
       on Beauty's shell
or failing that
       to try once more
for Wisdom's attention—
       bills   bones   teeth
coughed up as a pellet

I heard that trees communicate

with each other underground,
and I wonder what *WARNING*
sounds like when

they're about to be cut down.
Enter the gates of a new neighborhood
where trees lately stood. Try listening
for the echo

of language—a sound you'll not hear.
Or birds, foxes, deer. Gone is gone.
Where tract houses stitch horizon's
lips closed &

Studebakers once parked
in funerary rows, trees used to
flush secrets into roots, wiring codes
& intel like

spies tucking the brim of sky tight
against time. How upright &
efficient—to hold hidden hands,
hum, & die.

General Accident

Come sit with me a spell
and tell me good news   but if there's none
          we'll speak as we usually do   of horrible things
          Of events out of control spun
          Of forces once controlled now
not   Devoid as reason
flying standby
          In short: let us sit and do what we can
do

to admire the problem
          a phrase from Consulting   my first job at 22
          optimizing Claims for insurance companies
like *General Accident*

          I sat in a dolorous conference room
          windowless   bereft
of contact unless a resentful
Adjuster poked in to watch me spinning
his world with Excel
          data   faxes

          This was a different sitting   not a spell
          And neither was the sitting in taxis   at gates   on planes
for the flight back to Philly on Fridays
          I was always pulling something behind me

          Like a black bulb   my bag dragged
a sac of venom/eggs/silk to stand by   wait with   wonder
sometimes aloud that I had such spinning
at my disposal   a gift gotten from seeming nowhere
          Such turns of web
          Such phrase of turn
          And I forced my horrible mouth to shape

thanks to a flirty Agent for the upgrade
      for a spell from proportion   logic until

a horrible thing came crawling out
      caught now   interposing
as a fly buzzing and we   it and I   talked then
of nothing   whirring of wings   of sky   before we flew
      fed on the sound of each other
going
gate after gate treading   wrapping
seatbelts around what we did
do in DKNY black suits
that came with a skirt and pants but only one jacket
cut for men
      Controlling who we
      Whir
      Speak   Sit   a spell

Meat Cookie Lady

Fathom that some man
authored the first witch:
a wild woman bestowed of

pitiless superpowers,
fearsome & fiery.

And how'd he characterize her?

Stirring a pot & muttering.
To be fair, it was unlikely
to have been just one man

but many bards traipsing over
Roman hill & Anglo-Saxon dale,

repeating & tweaking across centuries.

Their collective efforts yielding:
a line cook in a creative kitchen.
A wrinkled crone

saucing racks of toad ribs,
fork-scoring hedgehog hides,

& julienning newt bits—

patriarchal imagination
limited to a cauldron's dimensions.
Let's be the type of witch who

sympathizes with the cauldron,
—sinew to slime—,

forced to contain

whatever's considered
appalling . . .
. . . My old piano teacher

frightened me worse
than any hag, but

it was her bowl that did it—

steaming, unseasoned,
greige-toned meat
crouched within—

& she palmed the hot vessel
like a pagan offering

as she sat beside me on the bench,

shoulder-slapping with
the back of her other hand,
keeping tempo as blue light flickered

from a TV in the other room
where her husband LaZBoy-reclined,

watching *M*A*S*H* in his undershirt.

What precisely her bowl contained
I did not know, but my sister & I
called it a Meat Cookie when we

clambered into our Honda
at the end of the lesson,

competing for funniest anecdote of the hour.

Dad laughed & egged us on—
Meat Cookie Lady & LaZBoy
tossed into our boiling stew,

& when we quit piano—
because Mom finally caved,

having heard enough myth

about LaZBoy's hands down his pants,
Meat Cookie Lady's fetid breath,
& our stilted command

of the treble clef, *Practice*,
Meat Cookie Lady had intoned,

before penciling homework assignments

into our music books,
& the following week,
we showed back up,

not having practiced,
piano squatting black & heavy

before us, the burnt stub of middle C

forlorn in its center,
& told her we were through—
she knew it was coming.

Even as she wished us well,
Meat Cookie Lady's countenance said,

You cannot escape.

Practice these notes,
on these keys, in these rooms,
telling these tales to keep time, or

don't. One day, you'll hold
ingredients in your palm, smiling as you stir—

lank hair framing your steamed face,

unaware that the cauldron
hums a bubbling song as it plays you.

How the Crone Beckons

. . . Come near.
        You're here: map's edge

behind the box stamped *Legend.*
        Heart Repair's on the sign,

but it's equal parts gumption
        & gold inside. O, you're welcome to try:

pick up your pieces alone. But
        I've seen us circle & circle

the loop of our limits—dogs
        coming out of tail-chasing spins

dizzy on the dot. Whimper & groan
        against the rim of life's chipped

porcelain or get a handle on Doubt
        & tuck your pout. No more

lapping at the lake of Permission &
        I see Luck took a shortcut,

leaving you deserted . . .
        . . . That pained expression's familiar—

cracked, crazed with chagrin
        like Achilles' heel spread north

as a virulent Staph—heart-high
        then up to mouth.

Silly our moms forgot
        to flip us upside down & dip

for good measure. O, jot down
            her name if it helps,

but the river will return her
            —Your Mom—

to Sender: bedraggled, clutching
            your soggy Shit List

& calling it a present . . .
            . . . Neither swimmer nor stone,

step into my home, my hut,
            my hovel, my squat—

my comfortable lot in a life that's won
            one implausible boon:

I turn Grief into gold.
            Harm heels here

at my humble threshold. Someday's
            arrived in the stipple & skim

of brushes tracing, bracing
            Broken with Better.

What was Weak within
            giggles, a trifle

ticklish—. Dear heart,
            wild bowl, hold . . .

            . . . Your gift: an audacious vein.
Both open & closed.

I remember, I remember

being 5 or 6 & pushing my toy shopping cart up the driveway, cooing to Broccoli in the baby seat—its green, bulbous head riding high. Mom never participated in this game, likely using the moment as a respite for a bath or clandestine smoke out back.

I clutched my little plastic pockabook, feeling nearly desperate to pay in oak leaves & acorns if I could persuade Dad to idle the lawnmower & ring me up at the tree stump cash register. He always seemed put out, which I chalked up to theatrical commitment.

One day, I parked my cart & went inside for something—a drink of water or to use the bathroom. I told Broccoli to *Sit tight, don't touch anything*—wagging my finger—*be nice to Meat & Milk*. When I came out, Dad was wielding a sledgehammer there in the garage, backlit by midday sun. He raised the hammer & brought it down on my shopping cart. It buckled then gave out. Again & again, he swung until it lay on the cement slab like a child's toy broken.

To say this is my earliest memory when someone asks, *What's your earliest memory?*;
to say Mom came screaming out of the house, held me tight to her body;
to say I heard his name repeated as though it were partner to the hammer;
to say he bent down, turned me around, & touched my head as he said, *I'll buy you another one*;
to say I told my sister the other day about this poem & she replied, *You're wrong, it was a wagon*.

To say so is to push the squeaky wheel of litany a little faster down Aisle 6, forever Aisle 6, calling for the Clean-up of Conciliation, the Mop of Advice:

> Start your shopping from the outer aisles where items
> are healthier then work your way in; never leave your
> purse unattended or turn your back on a child in the
> seat; & if you drop an Orange or Head of Broccoli on
> the floor, the right thing to do is:

> A) Mutter a wistful apology to no one in
>   particular, pick it up, & bury it among
>   the others;

> B) See who's looking, laugh together, then
>   bag it & pay;

> C) Both. Both.

Ball Game

I like to think of the geologic timeline of planet Earth as a Cracker Jack box layered like an elaborate parfait where each era's biggest jokester buried a time capsule and if we dig ages later we might find, say, a Lego, fallen in beside peanuts, heavier than popcorn, settled toward the middle above arrowheads and Bronze Age artifacts, Viking sod hut outlines and backfill made of oyster shells, well past Easter Island monoliths shaped like those mugs with exaggerated faces all the way down to the brown bottom where a thin prize hides its hieroglyphic joke. The whole snack makes us hungrier than when we began because nostalgia isn't filling, it only raises more questions the way ethnographers, never satiated, studied only themselves while they jotted assiduously about the other and baseball was here before we had a mortgage or plastic and nobody ate a whole box alone ever and I don't know why I feel compelled to hold the box up to my mouth and tap the last dust in I cough every time and the flavor becomes the smell-flavor-smell of cardboard pulp and Phan-A-Vision where we hope to see ourselves see ourselves and I love the Phanatic so much it hurts when he drives his four-wheeler away and night bursts the field greener with city skyline behind a dream so aquatic the way thousands of people cheer and flare like schools of similar fish in colors against blue deep water and the memory of three peanuts rationed that if I hadn't eaten them might have spelled out a truth like a lot of this used to be ocean a historical rune lined up in my palm like breath blowing dirt from a fossil buried eons ago like everyone waving their foam fingers to the parking lot where their wheeled box waits to shake them home

Fluorescent Mammals

Here I am, a child of the '80s
just biding *One Day at a Time*, waiting
for Schneider, my building's hapless super,
to show up sheepishly wielding
the ultimate boon: one bulb of black light.

If I've got to die soon,
I wanna bear the Hedonists out.
Take me & submerge me—
tawny pelted & supremely average—
in blacklight where I guarantee I'll
tie dye & astound.

Elysian fields gotta bloom somewhere.
Why not at home? Except to say that
humans made Elysium up,
sending our measly derricks
plumb down & springhares invented this:
secret libraries erected in open air—
paper-marbled volumes spiraled sky high
from ground to whiskered cornice.

My life had stood a pastoral poem
green & pristine. Undiscovered glens
waiting for a hippie with a tab to
find them or a medicine woman
with mortar & pestle to grind them.

Meanwhile, springhares wear
Jupiter's clouds as hidden skin &
platypuses have settled in, gliding past
permission & pictures.
They're out here living—
dancing to music subdermal,

platypussing through midnight
water, emerging beaded
in flamboyant kit.

River-glittered Janus—
she knows it's last call,
boogies on her plot,
bucks up her bill,
& shoots her shot.
I want to go with her.
I want to go.
To a place where what swirls beneath
our surface is only:
                    B E T T E R
Signifying
nothing other than fuck it—
let's be beautiful in this tangle
of roots together.

In darkness, I watch her
bright body course, streak,
& dart. Her expression flickers.
I'm a mirror.
What's here is there,
within, without. Whether we're
colorful ENOUGH
is an absurd question.
Head to toe, we're animals
efflorescent—bodypainted
in poetry underneath
selfsame coats.

some people know what to say after death.

when someone's died and they're
standing beside the bed/casket/dug ground. some know what token to send
or withhold, foods that succor versus what will sit in the sunken hull
of the grief-stricken, their bottomed-out gut scraping beside their heart,
a useless cannon. some love to be useful/industrious/central
to reheating casseroles in the kitchen. we let that woman
outdo herself before retreating to the living room where the dead
one's rattling around, gawping at her unexpected company,
rushing to basket her knitting. that's maybe why they ghost. ghosting's
the done thing for the dead who don't know the etiquette. it takes a while
before they figure out—kids do funerals best. kids play, finding
a way beneath tables/down to the rec room/out of doors as they do
on a usual day. then they go to bed and dream of ghosts who stand
silent/solemn by their bedside, holding vigil over the vital.

Girl Icarus

On undulant ocean   Icarus lay
Tallow wings sizzled   formed

a raft that bore her
upon crested waves to land

Icarus strode   curling broken arches
over crushed stones   stumbling

because falling fractures
fragile bones

Icarus lazed
beneath bowered lemons   savoring olives

hearing healing
knit

tallow drip
by olive pit

Sky   meets   sea   in   a   line   as   thin   as   decision

as soft as lemon pith   as hard as falling   flapping
pliant wings against leaden air

losing loft   letting go
tumbling chance from

a dragging undertow

O

wingless seed   marooned stone
if held   if held   if

you hold yourself
high   close one eye

you can
eclipse sun

NOTES

Epigraphs—potentially stabilizing formal gestures—are not generally used in this book, especially where poems respond to works of art by male creators.

Section titles reference stages of "the heroine's journey." The problematic gap between "The Queen" and "The Crone" is solved here by the addition of a new stage: "The Maven." Akin to the Campbellian hero's experience in the "Master of Two Worlds" stage, The Maven achieves balance between the material and the spiritual, moving freely as a powerful consultant. With integrated powers, The Maven enacts leadership electively yet easily while still living among those she'd previously served. This differs from The Queen, who embodies a self-sacrificing and relational stage about caring for and leading others for the betterment of the collective. She is also different from The Crone, who (in the extant archetype) moves herself to the edge of "the kingdom" in sardonic, if not cynical, isolation. The Maven already possesses The Crone's internal powers—imbued with holistic beauty and worldly wisdom—but she effervesces; having endured the rigors of earlier stages, The Maven personifies a heroine's apogee: fabulous wherewithal.

René Magritte allusions: "Self-Portrait with Bubble Gum" and "The Daughter of Man" triptych respond to Magritte's *The Son of Man* (1946), and my "Empire of Fire" to his *Empire of Light* (1953–1954).

"15 Minutes" alludes to pop artist Andy Warhol's quip about fame's duration; the 1969 Apollo 11 moon landing; Kirk Gibson's 1988 World Series Game One walk-off home run; Michael Jackson's 1984 Grammy Award performance of "Billie Jean," which included the moonwalk; and frozen TV dinners. The final line alludes to T. S. Eliot's "The Love Song of J. Alfred Prufrock": "I have measured out my life with coffee spoons."

"Afterschool Special Rewound" includes many pop culture allusions and references to commercial products. ABC, the television network, aired "Afterschool Specials" (1972–1997)—scripted, hour-long moralizing stand-alones confronting teenage social issues. Doritos are a triangular snack chip; Formica is a laminate product often used as a kitchen countertop surface; the Breathalyzer is a blood-alcohol-level measuring device; Atari was a home video game console, and one of its obstacle-course games was called *Pitfall*; and Mad Libs are a fill-in-the-blank word game. The Presidential Physical Fitness Test was a federally mandated athletic challenge completed in school gym class, and one of the exercises for girls was the "flexed arm hang"—an isometric pull-up. Spin-the-Bottle is a "wheel of fortune" game played as a sexual rite of passage, designed to yield transactional kissing amongst players. Old Maid is a card game in which the loser ends holding the card depicting an old, unmarried woman. Ouija boards allow players to make ostensible contact with the dead.

Trapper Keepers are Velcro-enclosable academic notebooks. Brownies are junior Girl Scouts, ages seven to nine, and Thin Mints are a cookie variety they sell. The slogan first developed and championed in 1984 by First Lady Nancy Reagan and her anti-drug-use campaign for teens appears here. The poem also alludes to T. S. Eliot's "The Love Song of J. Alfred Prufrock" in referencing "Michelangelo": "In the room the women come and go / Talking of Michelangelo." Robert Frost's poem "Nothing Gold Can Stay" is quoted, perhaps most intentionally for its use in S. E. Hinton's 1967 novel *The Outsiders*.

"Ball Game" references the Philadelphia Phillies; Citizens Bank Park; the team's mascot, the Phanatic; and PhanaVision, the stadium video screen. Cracker Jacks, the traditional ballpark snack of caramel popcorn and peanuts packed in a pulp box, and LEGO, the plastic toy brick, are also referenced.

"Barnegat Light" mentions Tawny Kitaen (1961–2021), a model and '80s music video star.

"Date Rape" is in conversation with Christopher Salerno's "Headfirst," which begins with this line: "Just a boy then, I was struck."

"The Daughter of Man" refers to Uncle Sam, the patriotic persona of wartime recruitment, including the finger-pointing "I want you" campaign.

"Everything's Elegy" alters a line from Walt Whitman's "Song of Myself," 6: "And to die is different from what anyone supposed, and luckier." Characters from Sophocles' *Antigone* and William Shakespeare's *King Lear* are also mentioned.

"Fluorescent Mammals" alters a line from Emily Dickinson's "My Life had stood—a Loaded Gun" (764) and refers to a television sitcom, *One Day at a Time* (1975–1984). The poem was inspired by a *New York Times* article written by Cara Giaimo, "Meet the Newest Member of the Fluorescent Mammal Club" (February 18, 2021).

"General Accident" is in conversation with Robert Frost's "Design" and alludes to a line from Jefferson Airplane's "White Rabbit": "When logic and proportion / have fallen sloppy dead." The title refers to an insurance-company project on which I was staffed as an analyst with Andersen Consulting in the late '90s. DKNY (Donna Karan New York) was a source for contemporary professional clothing.

"How the Crone Beckons" was inspired by the Japanese art of kintsugi: repairing broken pottery with gold instead of glue, which serves to highlight rather than conceal the object's history of damage.

"I heard that trees communicate" references automobiles produced by the popular American manufacturer Studebaker, which once enjoyed commercial ubiquity.

"I remember, I remember" was inspired by Thomas Hood's poem of the same title.

"Kristallnacht," or "the night of broken glass," occurred on November 9–10, 1938, in Nazi Germany. Assault and vandalism were enacted against Jewish people and their businesses on this infamous night. In the aftermath, Germany became more restrictive toward its Jewish citizens; for example, female Jews who did not have "typically Jewish" given names were forced to add "Sara" to official identification cards as of January 1939. My grandmother Lotte Strauss (1913–2020) and her story—of flight across the Swiss border from Germany with my grandfather Herbert A. Strauss (1918–2005) and their ultimate arrival in New York City in 1946—served as inspiration. This story can be found in their respective memoirs: *Over the Green Hill: A German Jewish Memoir, 1913–1943* and *In the Eye of the Storm: Growing Up Jewish in Germany, 1918–1943* (both published by Fordham University Press, 1999). This poem also owes a debt to ee cummings' "maggie and milly and molly and may."

"Landscape with Wisteria" sprang from a misreading of the first line of Ruth Stone's "So What," which reads, "For me the great truths are laced with hysteria." My poem also references physicists Albert Einstein (as does Stone's poem) and Isaac Newton.

"Like Poetry" alters a phrase from the first stanza of T. S. Eliot's "The Wasteland" ("stirring / Dull roots") and also references TikTok, a social media platform, and King Kong, the sympathetic "monster" from the 1933 film (directed by Merian C. Cooper).

"The Mall" was inspired by James Wright's "Beginning" and borrows its first sentence almost faithfully: "The moon drops one or two feathers into the field." Two mainstream '80s women's fashion designers, Gloria Vanderbilt and Evan Picone, are mentioned.

"Meat Cookie Lady" refers to *M*A*S*H* (1972–1983), a CBS television show about American doctors and nurses serving near the front during the Korean War; and La-Z-Boy, a furniture company specializing in reclining chairs.

"M.I.L.F." is an acronym for "Mother I'd Like to Fuck," a contemporary colloquialism; a Ford F-150 is a pickup truck of American manufacture.

"The Mooning 1986 (Etiology of the Cauldron)" was inspired by Galway Kinnell's "Hide-and-Seek 1933," which begins with this line: "Once when we were playing."

"Pleasure in the Age of Overwhelm" alludes to Gerard Manley Hopkins' "God's Grandeur" and the song "America the Beautiful."

"Plinko" references the popular game on the CBS television game show *The*

Price Is Right (particularly the Bob Barker–hosted version that ran from 1972–2007) in which a token pinged down a pegged board to land in a prize-labeled slot. It also references Tang, a juice product with an astronaut-themed TV ad campaign; and Broyhill, a furniture-company sponsor.

"Pockabook" references Binaca and Velamints, both breath fresheners, and Goody hairbrushes. Jackie O sunglasses were oversized round black frames made famous by former First Lady Jacqueline Kennedy Onassis (1929–1994). Red Rover is an outdoor, two-team game in which players form a line by holding hands or wrists, summon an opposing player with a chant, and receive that player, who runs at the line and against / into their arms—painfully. If the line breaks, the player returns "home," but if the line holds, the player joins the "enemy."

"Pool" owes a debt to both James Wright's "Lying in a Hammock at William Duffy's Farm in Pine Island, Minnesota" and David Hockney's *A Bigger Splash* (1967).

"prom" is in conversation with Marcel Duchamp's *Nude Descending a Staircase (No. 2)* (1912).

"scherenschnitte" references German "scissor art" in which artists use white paper and scissors to render pastoral scenes. My grandmother's story served as inspiration (see note for "Kristallnacht").

"Self-Portrait as Molly Pitcher" refers to colonial personages Molly Pitcher and Betsy Ross (1752–1836). Pitcher, or some amalgam of women, may have brought water to thirsty soldiers at the Battle of Monmouth in New Jersey in June 1778; Ross, a seamstress, is said to have helped design and sew the new American flag in Philadelphia, Pennsylvania, in 1776.

"Self-Portrait with Bubble Gum" makes mention of Hubba Bubba bubble gum, Lucky Charms cereal, *TV Guide* magazine, Sweet 'n Low sugar substitute, Ray-Ban sunglasses, and *National Geographic* magazine, particularly the June 1985 cover photo by Steve McCurry of "the girl with the eyes"—an Afghan girl later identified as Sharbat Gula.

"some people know what to say after death." owes a debt to Ellen Bryant Voigt's "My Mother," especially for the "casserole" and the "succor."

"Surface Tension" references *The Wizard of Oz* (directed by Victor Fleming, 1939), Crayola crayon colors, and the Powerball lottery.

"tablescape" mentions Busby Berkeley (1895–1976), the American film director and choreographer famous for musical numbers in which female dancers' bodies, especially their legs, formed complex, abstract moving shapes.

"To the hypothetical hostile man in the audience:" makes use of the September 2016 speech in which former secretary of state and presidential candidate Hillary Clinton characterized ("half") her opponent's supporters as "a basket of deplorables."

"Trees and paint aren't different," makes reference to: musical artists Donna Summer, Stevie Nicks, and Nirvana, quoting lyrics (or the title) from their songs "Bad Girls" (1979), "Edge of Seventeen" (1981), and "Smells Like Teen Spirit" (1991), respectively; two alcoholic products—Jägermeister, a potent black-licorice-flavored German liqueur, and Pabst Blue Ribbon, an American beer; William Shakespeare's *Macbeth*; and the American abstract expressionist / action painter Jackson Pollock (1912–1956).

"'Trompe L'Oeil" translates to "trick of the eye." Allusions include the ceiling of the Ducal Palace in Mantua, painted by Andrea Mantegna (1431–1506); Magritte's *The Treachery of Images* (*Ceci n'est pas une pipe*); *Escaping Criticism* by Pere Borrell del Caso (1835–1910); and the Chatsworth House violin by Jan van der Vaardt (1650–1727).

The "What a Warrior Whispers" triptych responds to works by Artemisia Gentileschi (1593–1656). The first poem in this series considers Gentileschi's late-career *Self-Portrait as the Allegory of Painting* (1638–1639), which depicts Gentileschi in the act of painting. An accomplished artist, Gentileschi received limited training due to sexism, though she had early access via her father, who was a disciple of Caravaggio. The second poem in the series responds to *Judith Beheading Holofernes* (ca. 1620). An Assyrian invader, Holofernes was beheaded by a temptress named Judith whose female servant, Abra, aided her effort. Gentileschi completed her version of this oft-painted subject in the aftermath of her rape by a painting tutor. An ensuing trial—complete with finger torture, which was a lie-detector precursor, and gynecological exams—made the victim a pariah. The final poem in the series responds to *Susanna and the Elders* (1610). The painting of a nude female crouching below two male figures may allude to an episode in Gentileschi's early biography in which her nudity was treated as the source of scandal by local townsmen. Despite these obstacles, Gentileschi achieved both financial stability and critical recognition during her artistic career.

"What's stupid" refers to Bob's Big Boy, a hamburger restaurant chain founded in California in 1936; *Gunsmoke* (1955–1975), a television Western; and *Green Acres* (1965–1971), a television sitcom.

"The Yassification of Dolly Parton" refers to the famous singer-songwriter / actor / performer / philanthropist and her song "Jolene." The word "yassification" originated on Twitter and, in verb form, is defined as embellishing, gilding, stylizing, or otherwise boosting something.